Hassle - Free Puppy Food Cookbook

Healthy & Delicious Puppy Food Recipes
That Any Puppy Would Love

CW01496990

BY - Stephanie Sharp

wwwwwwwwwwwwwwwwwwwwwwwwwwwwwwww

License Notes

wwwwwwwwwwwwwwwwwwwwwwwwwwwwwwwwwwww

Table of Contents

Introduction

Would you like your dog to eat healthy, delicious food and treats fresh from your kitchen?

Dogs are just like humans. They need to be fed right so that they can live a longer, happy life. Packaged, readymade food is very convenient, but they are no comparison to natural homemade food.

When you cook for your dogs, you save them from the artificial sweetening agents and preservatives used in commercial food. Another benefit you derive from home cooking for your dog is it creates a special bond between you and your dog.

You will find over 30 simple dog treats and food recipes inside to feed your best friend. Nutritional requirements have been considered and the ingredients used in these recipes are readily available. You will also be shown a simple technique where you won't have to cook every day.

You will be informed of:

- The correct quantity of food your dog requires.
- What food is best to feed your dog.
- The ingredients to avoid when cooking for your dog.
- And many more.
- Get your copy now!

Dog Food Casserole

This is a healthy and savory dog food dish you can make any night of the week for your best friend. It makes so much; you can put some away for later.

Serves: 6

Time: 20 minutes

Ingredients:

- 3 cups of brown rice, cooked
- 4 Tablespoons of carrots, grated
- 4 Tablespoons of spinach, chopped
- ½ cup of non-fat cottage cheese
- 1 tablespoon of nutritional yeast
- ¼ cup of fat free milk
- ¼ cup of grated low-fat parmesan cheese

Directions:

1. Preheat the oven to 350 degrees.

2. In a casserole dish, add the cooked brown rice, grated carrots, chopped spinach, non-fat cottage cheese and nutritional yeast. Stir well to mix.

3. Add in the fat free milk and stir well to mix.

4. Sprinkle the grated parmesan cheese over the top.

5. Place into the oven to bake for 15 minutes or until golden.

6. Remove and cool completely before serving.

Slow Cooker Chicken

This is one of the best homemade dog food recipes you can make if you don't have the time to prepare dog food. It is made in a slow cooker, making it even easier to prepare.

Serves: 2 servings

Time: 6 to 8 hours

Ingredients:

- 4 chicken breasts, boneless and skinless
- ½ cup of green beans, chopped
- ½ cup of carrots, chopped
- ½ cup of broccoli, chopped
- ½ cup of rolled oats, optional
- 4 cups of water

Directions:

1. Add in your ingredients to your slow cooker. Stir gently to mix.

2. Cover and set to the lowest setting.

3. Cook for 6 to 8 hours.

4. Turn off the slow cooker.

5. Allow to cool completely before serving.

Multi-grain Dog Food

Grains contain various proteins and essential minerals that dogs can benefit from. Preparing this food is pretty straightforward and simple, it can be made in a matter of minutes.

Yield: 2 servings

Time: 50 minutes

Ingredients:

- 2 cups of whole wheat flour
- 1 ½ cup of all-purpose flour
- ½ cup of soy flour
- 1 cup of cornmeal
- 1 cup of powdered milk
- 1 cup of rolled oats
- ½ cup of wheat germ
- ½ cup of brewer's yeast
- 1 tablespoon of salt
- 1 egg
- 5 Tablespoons of corn oil
- 3 cups of water

Directions:

1. Preheat the oven to 350 degrees.

2. In a bowl, add in the whole wheat flour, all-purpose flour, soy flour, cornmeal, powered milk, rolled oats, wheat germ, dash of salt and brewer's yeast. Stir well to mix.

3. In a separate bowl, add the egg, corn oil and water. Whisk well until lightly beaten. Add into the flour mix. Stir well until incorporated.

4. Divide the dough onto two baking sheets and spread evenly.

5. Place into the oven to bake for 45 minutes. Remove and set aside to cool completely.

6. Break into small pieces of kibble and serve.

Simple Chicken and Vegetable Dinner

This is an easy and simple dinner dish that you can make for those picky pups in your home. It is made with chicken and healthy veggies such as cauliflower and carrots.

Serves: 2 servings

Time: 55 minutes

Ingredients:

- 2 chicken breasts, boneless and skinless
- ¼ cup of cauliflower, chopped into florets
- ¼ cup of carrots, chopped
- ¼ cup of squash, peeled and chopped
- ¼ cup of spinach
- 1 sweet potato, cooked
- 2 cups of brown rice

Directions:

1. In a saucepan set over medium heat to high heat, add in the chicken breasts. Cover the chicken breasts with water and allow to come to a boil. Boil for 20 minutes or until the chicken is cooked through.

2. Remove the chicken and set aside to cool completely.

3. Pour out enough of the water until you have 4 cups left. Add in the brown rice. Allow to come back to a boil. Lower the heat to and cook for 20 minutes or until the rice is cooked through.

4. Set your steamer basket over a pot of boiling water in medium heat, add in the cauliflower florets, chopped carrots, chopped squash and spinach. Steam for 5 minutes or until the vegetables are soft.

5. Scoop out the fresh of the sweet potatoes into a bowl. Beat in a mixer until creamy in consistency.

6. In the bowl, add in the chicken and steamed vegetables. Add in the cooked brown rice and stir well to evenly mix.

7. Set aside to cool completely before serving.

Peanut Butter Cereal Dog Food

This is another great tasting homemade dog food recipe you can make for those picky pups in your household.

Serves: 2 servings

Time: 6 to 8 hours

Ingredients:

- ¼ cup of honey crunch wheat germ cereal
- ½ cup of rolled oats
- 2 cups of whole wheat flour
- 2 teaspoons of pure vanilla
- 3 Tablespoons of smooth peanut butter
- ½ cup of fish oil
- 1 ½ cups of water
- ½ cup of cornmeal

Directions:

1. In a bowl, add in the cornmeal, rolled oats, whole wheat flour and honey crunch wheat germ cereal. Stir well to mix.

2. In in the fish oil, smooth peanut butter and water. Stir well until a soft dough begins to form.

3. Place the dough onto a floured surface. Roll until ¼ inch in thickness.

4. Slice the dough into bars. Transfer onto a baking dish.

5. Place into the oven to dehydrated at 140 degrees for 6 to 8 hours.

6. Once hard, remove and serve.

Apple Dog Cakes

This is a healthy and nutritious food to serve to your pups any night of the week. They are simple to make; you can have them ready in just a matter of a few minutes.

Serves: 2

Time: 1 hour and 20 minutes

Ingredients:

- 2 ¾ cups of water
- ¼ cup of unsweetened applesauce
- 2 Tablespoons of honey
- 1/8 Tablespoons of pure vanilla
- 1 egg
- 4 cups of whole wheat flour
- 1 cup of dried apple chips, unsweetened
- 1 tablespoon of baker's style baking powder

Directions:

1. Preheat the oven to 350 degrees.

2. In a bowl, add your water, unsweetened applesauce, honey, egg and pure vanilla. Stir well.

3. Toss in the whole wheat flour, unsweetened dried apple chips and baking powder then stir.

4. Pour the mix into greased muffin pans, filling each cup with space to rise.

5. Bake for 75 minutes or until baked through.

6. Remove and set aside to cool completely before serving.

Homemade Crunchy Dog Food

This is the perfect dog food to make whenever you want to give your dogs a bit of variety. Not only is this type of dog food healthier than most dog foods, but it is also less expensive to make as well.

Serves: 4

Time: 1 hour

Ingredients:

- 4 cups of whole wheat flour
- 2 cups of rye flour
- 2 cups of nonfat powdered milk
- 2 teaspoons of bone meal
- 1 cup of plain wheat germ
- ½ cup of parsley, chopped
- 1 teaspoon of salt
- 4 eggs
- 1 cup of safflower oil
- 4 Tablespoons of Worcestershire sauce
- 3 cups of water
- 4 cups of lean ground lamb, cooked
- 2 cups of sweet potatoes
- 1 ½ cups of dried apples, chopped
- 2 cups of spinach

Directions:

1. Preheat the oven to 300 degrees. Grease two cooking sheets with baking spray.

2. In a bowl, add in the powdered milk, whole wheat flour, rye flour, bone meal, plain wheat germ, chopped parsley and salt. Stir well to mix.

3. Combine your eggs and safflower oil. Stir well until smooth in consistency.

4. Toss in your Worcestershire sauce and stir until evenly incorporated. Pour into the flour mix until mixed.

5. Add your cooked ground lamb, chopped sweet potatoes, chopped dried apples and spinach. Stirring well to mix.

6. Spread the dough onto the two baking sheets to form an 18 inch rectangle. Slice into squares.

7. Bake until baked through (about an hour). Remove and set aside to cool completely.

8. Crumble the squares finely and serve.

Buffaloaf Dinner

This is a rich and high protein dog food dish that can be served to dogs with specific protein sensitivities. It is made with buffalo and will please even the pickiest of dogs.

Serves: 2 servings

Time: 45 minutes

Ingredients:

- 3 cups of lean and ground buffalo
- 2 eggs
- 1 ½ cups of old fashioned oats
- ¼ cup of zucchini, chopped
- ¼ cup of broccoli, chopped into florets
- ¼ cup of carrots, chopped
- ¼ cup of sweet potatoes, chopped

Directions:

1. Preheat the oven to 350 degrees.

2. In a bowl, add in the lean and ground buffalo, eggs, old fashioned oats, chopped zucchini, chopped broccoli florets, chopped carrots and chopped sweet potatoes. Stir well to mix.

3. Press the mix into a loaf pan. Press down slightly.

4. Bake for 40 minutes.

5. Remove and cool completely before serving.

Simple Beef and Rice Dinner

This is another delicious dinner dish that you can make whenever you need a simple and healthy dinner that you can make for your pup.

Serves: 2 servings

Time: 50 minutes

Ingredients:

- 1 pound of lean ground beef
- 2 cups of brown rice
- 5 cups of water
- 1 pack of frozen cauliflower florets
- ½ cup of carrots, chopped

Directions:

1. Set a saucepan over medium heat, add in 1 teaspoon of vegetable oil. Add in the lean ground beef. Cook until browned.

2. Add in the frozen cauliflower florets and chopped carrots.

3. Add in the brown rice and water. Stir well to incorporate.

4. Increase the heat to high. Allow to come to a boil. Lower heat then cook for 25 minutes on low.

5. Remove from heat and set aside to cool.

6. Shape the mix into balls and serve.

Dog Food Lamb Cake

This is a delicious lamb cake that you can serve to your dog if they are extremely picky. One bite and they will devour it in minutes.

Serves: 4

Time: 1 hour and 10 minutes

Ingredients:

- 3 cups of lean ground lamb
- 1 egg
- 1 cup of oatmeal
- ½ cup of almond meal
- 1 tablespoon of fat free cottage cheese
- Dog treats, crumbled
- Fat free cream cheese, as needed and optional

Directions:

1. Preheat the oven to 375 degrees.

2. In a blender, add in the ground lamb, egg, oatmeal, almond meal and fat free cottage cheese. Blend on the highest setting until evenly mixed.

3. Spoon the mix into a cake pan that has been greased with vegetable spray.

4. Bake until cooked through (an hour). Remove and let rest for 5 minutes.

5. Cool completely. Enjoy.

Homemade Beef Stew

Beef stew is not only a human favorite, but it is also a dog favorite recipe.

Serves: 2 servings

Time: 35 minutes

Ingredients:

- 1 pound of ground beef
- 1 sweet potato, chopped
- 1 carrot, chopped
- ½ cup of frozen peas
- Water, as needed

Directions:

1. Set your pot over medium heat, add in the ground beef. Cook until browned.

2. Add in the chopped sweet potato, chopped carrot and frozen peas. Stir well to mix.

3. Cover with as much water as needed.

4. Cover with a lid and allow to come to a boil. Lower the heat to low. Cook for 20 minutes at a simmer.

5. Switch off heat and cool completely before serving.

Turkey Kibble

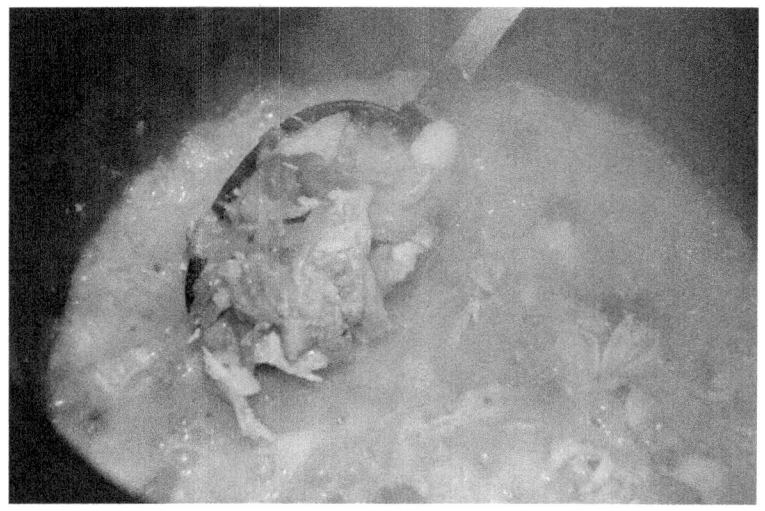

Make this homemade dog food for a dog that is suffering from food sensitivities. This is a recipe that works well if you need to travel with your dog.

Serves: 6 servings

Time: 2 hours

Ingredients:

- 8 ½ cups of whole wheat flour
- 2 cups of powdered nonfat milk
- 2 eggs
- ½ cup of extra virgin olive oil
- 1 pound of lean ground turkey
- 2 cups of sweet potato, cooked and pureed

Directions:

1. Preheat the oven to 200 degrees. Grease a cookie sheet with cooking spray.

2. In a bowl, add in the whole wheat flour, powdered dry milk, eggs and extra virgin olive oil. Stir well to mix.

3. Add in the ground turkey and pureed sweet potatoes. Stir well until smooth in consistency.

4. Place the dough onto a flat surface. Roll out the dough until it is ¼ inch in thickness. Transfer onto the cookie sheet.

5. Cut the dough into small kibble pieces.

6. Place into the oven to bake for 90 minutes. Turn off the oven and allow the kibble to cool completely.

7. Remove the kibble and cut into small pieces. Serve.

Vegetarian Miniature Muffins

While this particular dish can be fed to a dog as a treat, if you add chicken or beef instead, it can be a tasty meal for picky canines.

Serves: 2 servings

Time: 25 minutes

Ingredients:

- 1 apple, core removed and shredded
- 2 cups of carrots, shredded
- ¼ cup + 2 Tablespoons of molasses
- ¼ cup of water
- 1 cup of flax seed
- ¼ cup of dried oats
- ¾ cup of whole wheat flour

Directions:

1. Preheat the oven to 400 degrees.

2. In a bowl, add in the shredded apple, shredded carrots, molasses, water, flaxseed, dried oats and whole wheat flour.

3. Stir well to mix until a thick batter begins to form.

4. Pour the batter into a miniature muffin pan, fill each cup ¾ of the way full.

5. Place into the oven to bake for 15 minutes or until browned.

6. Remove and cool completely before removing.

Homemade Senior Dog Food

This is the perfect homemade dog food to make for senior pets. It is lower in protein and lower in fat.

Serves: 2 servings

Time: 15 minutes

Ingredients:

- ¼ pound of lean ground beef
- 2 cups of brown rice, cooked and no salt added
- 1 hardboiled egg, peeled and chopped
- 3 slices of white bread
- 1 teaspoon of powdered calcium carbonate

Directions:

1. Set your skillet over high heat, add your ground beef. Cook until browned.

2. Transfer into a bowl and set aside to cool completely.

3. in the bowl, add in the cooked brown rice, chopped hardboiled egg, slices of white bread and powdered calcium carbonate. Stir well to evenly mix.

4. Serve and store the excess for later.

Dog Chili

Just like human chili, this is the perfect chili dish for you to make for your dog during the cold winter months.

Serves: 4 servings

Time: 30 minutes

Ingredients:

- 4 chicken breasts, boneless and skinless
- 1 cup of kidney beans
- 1 cup of black beans
- 1 cup of carrots, chopped
- ½ cup of tomato paste
- 4 cups of chicken broth

Directions:

1. Trim the excess fat from the chicken breasts and chop into small pieces.

2. In a skillet set over medium to high heat, add in 1 teaspoon of fish oil. Add in the chicken breasts pieces. Cook for 8 to 10 minutes. Transfer into a soup pot.

3. In the soup pot, add in the drained kidney beans, drained black beans, chopped carrots, tomato paste and chicken broth. Stir well to mix. Cook over medium heat and cook for 10 minutes.

4. Remove and set aside to cool completely.

5. Serve.

Buffalo Hash

Buffalo is known for having a lower fat content than most protein sources used in homemade dog foods today. However, if you can't access buffalo, don't hesitate to use chicken or turkey instead.

Serves: 7 servings

Time: 15 minutes

Ingredients:

- 2 Tablespoons of extra virgin olive oil
- 1 pound of ground buffalo
- 2 eggs
- 2 cups of carrots, chopped
- 1 cup of peas, frozen
- 1 cup of celery, chopped
- 2 cups of brown rice, cooked

Directions:

1. Set your skillet over high heat with olive oil. Add in the ground buffalo. Cook for 10 minutes or until browned.

2. Drain the excess grease.

3. Add in the eggs, chopped carrots, frozen peas, chopped celery and cooked brown rice. Stir well to mix.

4. Cook for 3 minutes or until the eggs are cooked through.

5. Remove and set aside to cool completely before serving.

Fish Cake Dinner

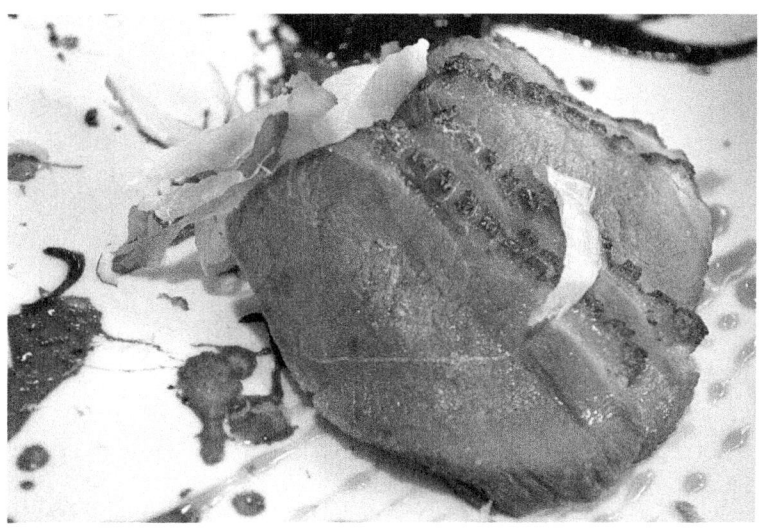

This is the perfect kind of dog food for you to make if you want to give your dog a shiny and healthy coat. Made with tuna, this is a dish that is packed full of healthy protein.

Serves: 2 servings

Time: 30 minutes

Ingredients:

- 2 potatoes
- 4 ounces of frozen peas
- 1, 15 ounce can of tuna
- 2, 15-ounce cans of albacore tuna
- 2 hardboiled eggs, chopped
- 1 handful of parsley, chopped

Directions:

1. Set a pot over medium heat, fill with water. Allow to come to a boil. Add in the potatoes. Boil for 20 minutes or until soft. Drain and set aside to cool completely. Transfer into a bowl and mash until smooth in consistency.

2. Add in ¼ of the chopped parsley and stir well to incorporate.

3. Prepare the frozen peas according to the directions on the package.

4. In a separate bowl, add in the cans of tuna and albacore tuna, the remaining parsley, chopped hardboiled eggs and prepared peas. Stir well to mix. Add in the mashed potatoes and stir again until evenly combined.

5. Set aside to cool completely before serving.

Salmon and Spinach Scramble

This dog food dish is packed full of omega 3 and 6 fatty acids which will leave your dog's coat nice and shiny.

Serves: 2 servings

Time: 10 minutes

Ingredients:

- 1 teaspoon of extra virgin olive oil
- ½ cup of spinach, chopped
- ½, 3 ounce can of salmon, boneless and drained
- 2 eggs

Directions:

1. Set your skillet over medium heat, add in the extra virgin olive oil.

2. Add in the chopped spinach and salmon. Cook until piping hot.

3. Add in the eggs and stir well to mix. Continue to cook for an additional 2 minutes or until the eggs are set.

4. Switch off heat then cool completely before serving.

Seafood Meatballs

This dish can be made for your dog whenever you want to help them achieve a shiny and healthy coat.

Serves: 4 servings

Time: 15 minutes

Ingredients:

- 2 pounds of frozen salmon fillets
- 1 to 2, 12-ounce cans of pink salmon
- ¼ to ½ pound of beef liver
- 1 to 3 eggs
- 1 cup of cabbage
- ¼ cup of broccoli florets
- ¼ cup of spinach
- ¼ cup of carrot, chopped
- ¼ cup of kale
- ½ cup of pumpkin seeds, shelled
- 2 Tablespoons of honey
- 2 Tablespoons of dried oregano
- 2 Tablespoons of dried parsley
- 2 Tablespoons of powdered turmeric
- 2 Tablespoons of powdered kelp

Directions:

1. In a meat grinder, add in the frozen salmon fillets, beef liver, pumpkin seeds, chopped carrot, cabbage, broccoli florets, kale and spinach. Grind into a bowl.

2. In the bowl, add in the honey, eggs, canned pink salmon, dried parsley, dried oregano, powdered turmeric and powdered kelp. Stir well to mix.

3. Shape the mix into meatballs.

4. If cooking the meatballs, place into a skillet. Cook until browned. Cool completely before serving.

5. Serve raw or cooked.

Miniature Pumpkin Muffins

This is a dish you should make if you have a dog with an upset stomach. Since it is made with pumpkin, it will help alleviate any diarrhea your dog may have.

Serves: 36 servings

Time: 25 minutes

Ingredients:

- 1 2/3 cups of rice flour
- 1 teaspoon of baker's style baking soda
- ½ teaspoons of powdered cinnamon
- 2 Tablespoons of molasses
- 1 ¾ cups of pureed pumpkin
- ½ cup of canola oil
- 2 eggs, beaten
- 1/3 cup of water

Directions:

1. Preheat the oven to 350 degrees. Grease a miniature muffin pan with cooking spray.

2. In a bowl, add in the rice flour, baker's style baking soda, powdered cinnamon and molasses. Stir well to mix.

3. Add in the pureed pumpkin, canola oil and egg. Add in the water. Stir until smooth in consistency.

4. Pour the mix into the muffin pan and complete the 2/3 cups of the way.

5. Place in the oven for 20 minutes or until it is baked.

6. Remove and cool completely before serving.

Chicken Casserole

Chicken is a fan favorite for nearly every dog. It is not only incredibly easy to prepare, but it is found in most homemade dog food recipes you will find.

Serves: 2 servings

Time: 55 minutes

Ingredients:

- 2 chicken breasts, boiled and chopped
- 1 cup of brown rice
- 1 cup of frozen peas
- 1 cup of carrots, steamed and chopped
- 1 cup of pureed pumpkin
- 1 stalk of celery, chopped
- 1 potato, boiled and chopped
- 3 Tablespoons of unsalted chicken broth

Directions:

1. Preheat the oven to 300 degrees.

2. Set your saucepan on medium to high heat, add in the chicken pieces. Pour enough water to cover. Allow to come to a saucepan. Cover and simmer for 30 minutes.

3. Set another saucepan on medium to high heat, add in the rice. Add in 2 cups of water.

4. Allow to come to a boil. Lower heat and simmer until the brown rice is cooked through (25 mins). Remove and set aside to cool completely.

5. In a bowl, add in the cooled brown rice, cooked chicken, peas, steamed carrots, pureed pumpkin, chopped celery and chopped potato. Stir well to mix. Pour into a baking dish.

6. Bake for 20 minutes.

7. Remove and cool completely before serving.

Growl Granola Bars

While traditional granola bars contain too much sugar to feed to dogs, this is a dish you can serve to your pups without any worry.

Serves: 36 servings

Time: 4 hours and 30 minutes

Ingredients:

- 3 ½ cups of old fashioned oats
- ½ teaspoons of powdered cinnamon
- 1 tablespoon of blackstrap molasses
- 1 cup of unsweetened peanut butter
- ¼ cup of water
- ½ cup of pureed pumpkin
- ¼ cup of applesauce
- ¼ cup of honey
- ¼ cup of dry roasted peanuts, chopped

Directions:

1. Preheat the oven to 350 degrees. Grease a baking dish with cooking spray.

2. In a bowl, add in all of the ingredients. Stir well until moist.

3. Press the mix into the greased baking dish.

4. Bake for 30 minutes.

5. Remove and place into the fridge to chill for 4 hours.

6. Slice into bars and serve.

Diarrhea All-in-One Mash

This is the perfect dish to help cure your dog's burst of diarrhea.

Serves: 2 servings

Time: 5 minutes

Ingredients:

- ½ cup of canned pumpkin
- 2 chicken breasts, boneless, skinless and boiled
- ½ cup of brown rice, cooked
- 2 Tablespoons of plain yogurt
- ¼ cup of warm water

Directions:

1. In a bowl, add in the cooked brown rice, canned pumpkin and plain yogurt. Stir well to mix.

2. Cut the boiled chicken into small pieces. Add in the warm water and stir well to mix. Add into the brown rice mix. Stir well until incorporated.

3. Serve immediately.

Fish and Veggie Patty

This patty is an absolute delight for most dogs. These patties are highly beneficial and will feed your dog the nutrients they require in order to thrive.

Serves: 4 servings

Time: 15 minutes

Ingredients:

- 1, 12 ounce can of salmon, in water
- 1 carrot, peeled and chopped
- 1 potato, peeled and chopped
- 1 egg
- 1 stalk of celery, chopped
- 3 Tablespoons of all-purpose flour
- Coconut oil, for frying

Directions:

1. Drain the can of salmon.

2. Add in the all-purpose flour and egg. Shape the salmon into small patties with your hands.

3. In a skillet set over medium to high heat, add in the coconut oil. Heat the oil to 350 degrees.

4. Add in the salmon patties. Fry until golden brown (5 mins). Remove and drain the patties on a plate lined with paper towels.

5. Serve the salmon patties with the chopped vegetables.

Arthritis Meal

If you have a dog that is currently suffering from arthritis, this is a recipe that is perfect for you. This is a food that is made with a variety of holistic ingredients that can help alleviate symptoms of arthritis.

Serves: 4 servings

Time: 7 hours and 20 minutes

Ingredients:

- 1 pound of white turkey meat
- 1 pound of extra lean ground beef
- ½ cup of brown rice, cooked
- ½ cup of carrots, thinly sliced
- ½ cup of kale
- ½ cup of celery, chopped
- ½ cup of cottage cheese
- ½ cup of peas
- ½ cup of broccoli, cut into florets
- ½ cup of green beans
- 1 cup of rolled oats
- 1 teaspoon of powdered alfalfa
- Dash of parsley, chopped
- 1 capsule of flaxseed oil
- 3 Tablespoons of unsalted beef broth

Directions:

1. In a slow cooker, add in the white turkey meat. Cook on the lowest setting for 7hours or until the turkey has an internal temperature of 145 degrees.

2. Cool the turkey and chop into small pieces.

3. In a skillet set over medium to high heat, add in the ground beef. Cook until browned. Transfer into a bowl to cool completely.

4. In the bowl, add in the cooked brown rice, 3 tablespoons of warm water, powdered alfalfa, green beans, broccoli florets, peas, cottage cheese, chopped celery, kale, sliced carrots, rolled oats, cooked turkey meat, flaxseed oil, beef broth and chopped parsley. Stir well to mix.

5. Cool completely before serving.

Chicken Thigh and Zucchini

This tasty dish will leave your pup even more in love with you.

Serves: 4

Time: 25 min

Ingredients:

- 1 lb. of skinned and boned chicken thighs
- One handful of basil (chopped)
- Two cups of thinly sliced zucchini
- Two tablespoons of coconut oil

Directions:

1. Pour oil into a medium skillet on medium heat.

2. Place your chicken thighs in hot oil and cook.

3. Turn over each side to cook for about six to eight minutes.

4. Remove chicken and shred or slice before returning the pieces into the pan.

5. Add your basil and zucchini and cook and stir occasionally for five minutes.

Chicken and Spinach

This Chicken and Spinach dish is easy to whip up and your pup will love it.

Serves: 4

Time: 35 min

Ingredients:

- 1 lb. of chicken breasts
- Three cups of spinach
- One teaspoon of ground turmeric
- 2 tablespoons of oil (olive or coconut)
- 1/8 teaspoon of black pepper

Directions:

1. Set your skillet over medium heat and pour in some oil.

2. Allow the oil to heat up.

3. Place chicken breasts into hot oil and cook for about ten minutes.

4. Flip over the chicken and cook another side for another ten minutes.

5. Remove the chicken and shred or slice.

6. Return chicken pieces back into the pan and pour in the pepper and turmeric.

7. Pour in spinach and stir. Then allow cooking for two minutes.

Pork and Butternut Squash

Enjoy this Butternut Squash and Pork dish will make a tasty dish for your best friend.

Serves: 4

Time: 40 min

Ingredients:

- 1 lb. of pork chops
- Two cups of cubed butternut squash
- 2 tablespoons of oil (olive or coconut)

Directions:

1. Place a medium skillet over medium heat.

2. Pour in your pork chops and allow to cook for about five to seven minutes.

3. Turn the pork chops over and pour in your butternut squash.

4. Cook for ten to twelve minutes with the skillet covered.

5. Remove pork chops and slice them into bite pieces.

6. Serve your dog and save the rest for later.

Steak and Sweet Potato

This Steak and Sweet Potato dish is a brilliant dinner and is extremely easy to make.

Serves: 3

Time: 30 min

Ingredients:

- 1 lb. of cubed sirloin steak
- One sprig of rosemary leaves
- 2 tablespoons of oil (olive or coconut)
- Two cups of peeled and cubed sweet potato

Directions:

1. Place a medium skillet over medium heat.

2. Pour in your sweet potato and cover it.

3. Cook for ten minutes.

4. Pour in your rosemary and steak and cover allowing to cook for another ten minutes while stirring often.

Turkey and Carrots

Serve up this Turkey and Carrot dish to your pup for dinner on any night of the week.

Serves: 4

Time: 25 min

Ingredients:

- 1 lb. of lean ground turkey
- Two cups of sliced carrots
- One teaspoon of thyme leaves
- Two tablespoons of olive or coconut oil

Directions:

1. Place a medium skillet over medium and place your turkey in the hot oil.

2. Use a spatula to break the turkey.

3. Pour in and stir your carrots.

4. Cook for ten to fifteen minutes and stir often.

5. Check that the meat is cooked through and stir in your thyme.

6. Serve as desired.

Conclusion

I hope you enjoyed preparing all 30 healthy & delicious puppy food recipes that any puppy would love. The aim of this Puppy Food Cookbook was to help you get closer to your amazing pup while providing them with healthy yet tasty meals.

If you enjoyed this journey through puppy land as much as I did, feel free to take a little time out to leave a review on the platform on which you purchased this cookbook.

Have a great night.

About the Author

Born in New Germantown, Pennsylvania, Stephanie Sharp received a Masters degree from Penn State in English Literature. Driven by her passion to create culinary masterpieces, she applied and was accepted to The International Culinary School of the Art Institute where she excelled in French cuisine. She has married her cooking skills with an aptitude for business by opening her own small cooking school where she teaches students of all ages.

Stephanie's talents extend to being an author as well and she has written over 400 e-books on the art of cooking and baking that include her most popular recipes.

Sharp has been fortunate enough to raise a family near her hometown in Pennsylvania where she, her husband and children live in a beautiful rustic house on an extensive piece of land. Her other passion is taking care of the furry members of her family which include 3 cats, 2 dogs and a potbelly pig named Wilbur.

Watch for more amazing books by Stephanie Sharp coming out in the next few months.

Author's Afterthoughts

I am truly grateful to you for taking the time to read my book. I cherish all of my readers! Thanks ever so much to each of my cherished readers for investing the time to read this book!

With so many options available to you, your choice to buy my book is an honour, so my heartfelt thanks at reading it from beginning to end!

I value your feedback, so please take a moment to submit an honest and open review on Amazon so I can get valuable insight into my readers' opinions and others can benefit from your experience.

Thank you for taking the time to review!

Stephanie Sharp

For announcements about new releases, please

follow my author page on Amazon.com!

You can find that at:

https://www.amazon.com/author/stephanie-sharp

*or Scan **QR-code** below.*

Printed in Great Britain
by Amazon

80968198R10048